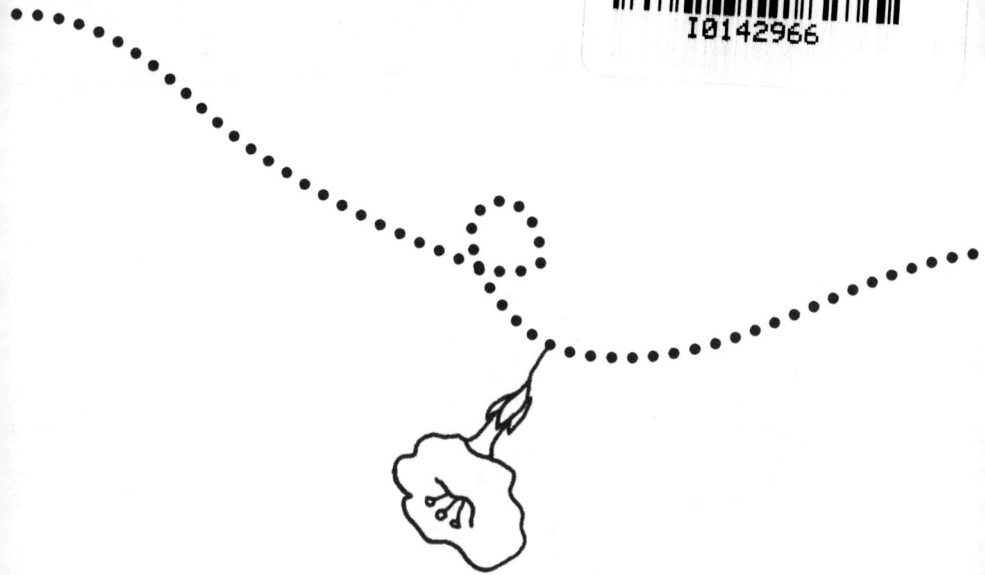

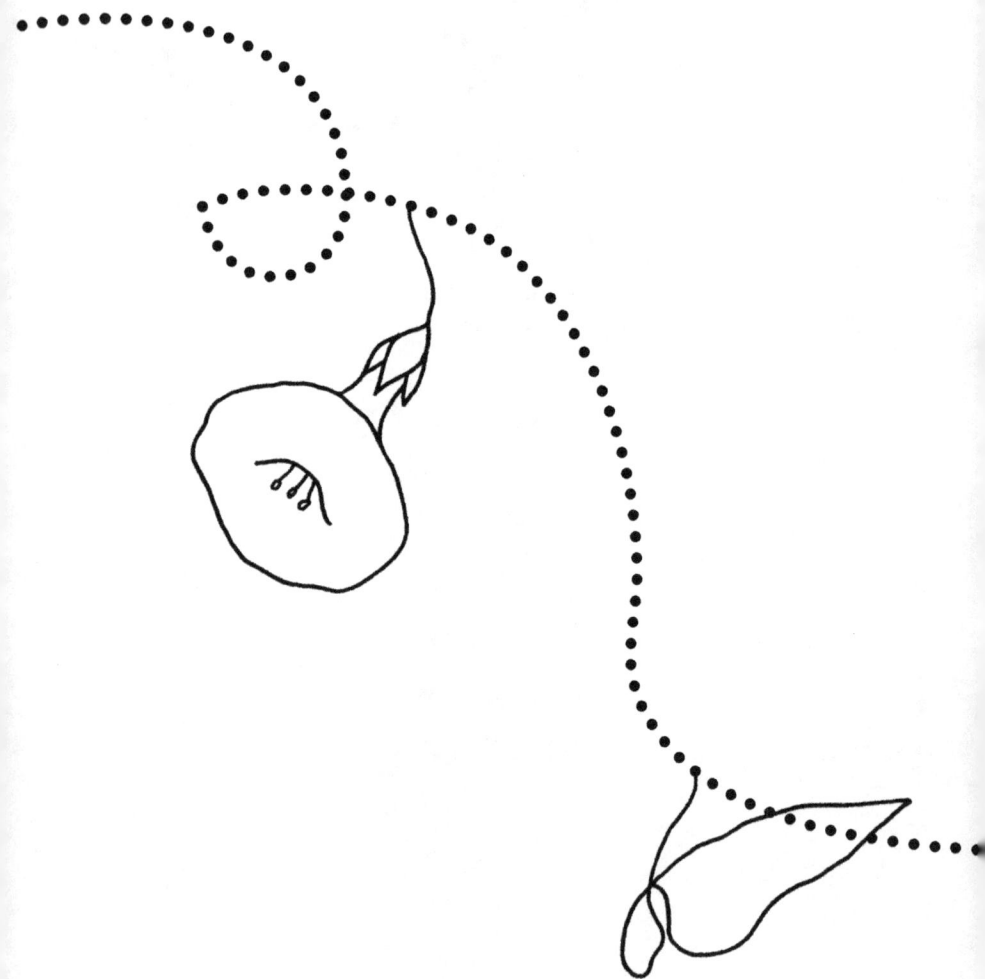

ident

poems by Alan John Stubbs

The Onslaught Press

Published in Oxford by The Onslaught Press
11 Ridley Road, OX4 2QJ
November 2016

☥

ISBN: 978-0-9956225-4-8

Typeset in Jean François Porchez's **Le Monde Livre** & **Le Monde Sans** inside,
with Oswald Bruce Cooper's **Cooper Black** on the cover & title page
Designed & edited by **Mathew Staunton**

Printed & bound by Lightning Source

Poems in *ident* have been published in:

The News and Star newspaper, Carlisle.
The Journal poetry magazine.
The book *To Kingdom Come*, Onslaught 2016
The Dawntreader, poetry magazine.
The Cannon's Mouth poetry magazine

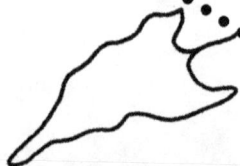

To Mum and Dad with Love

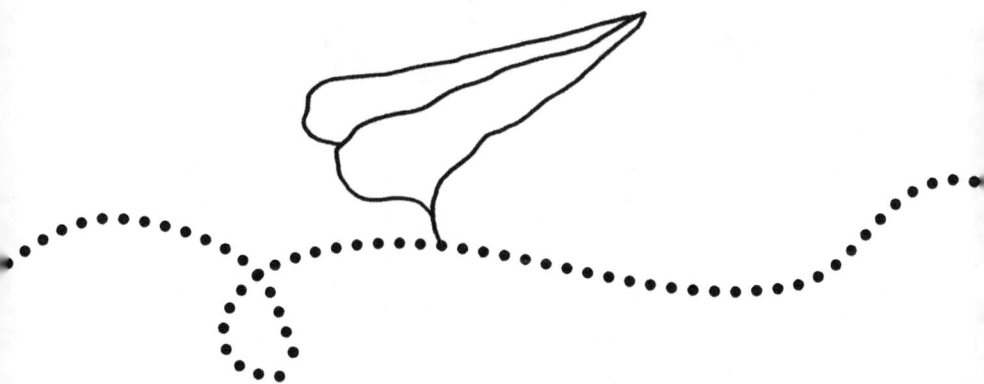

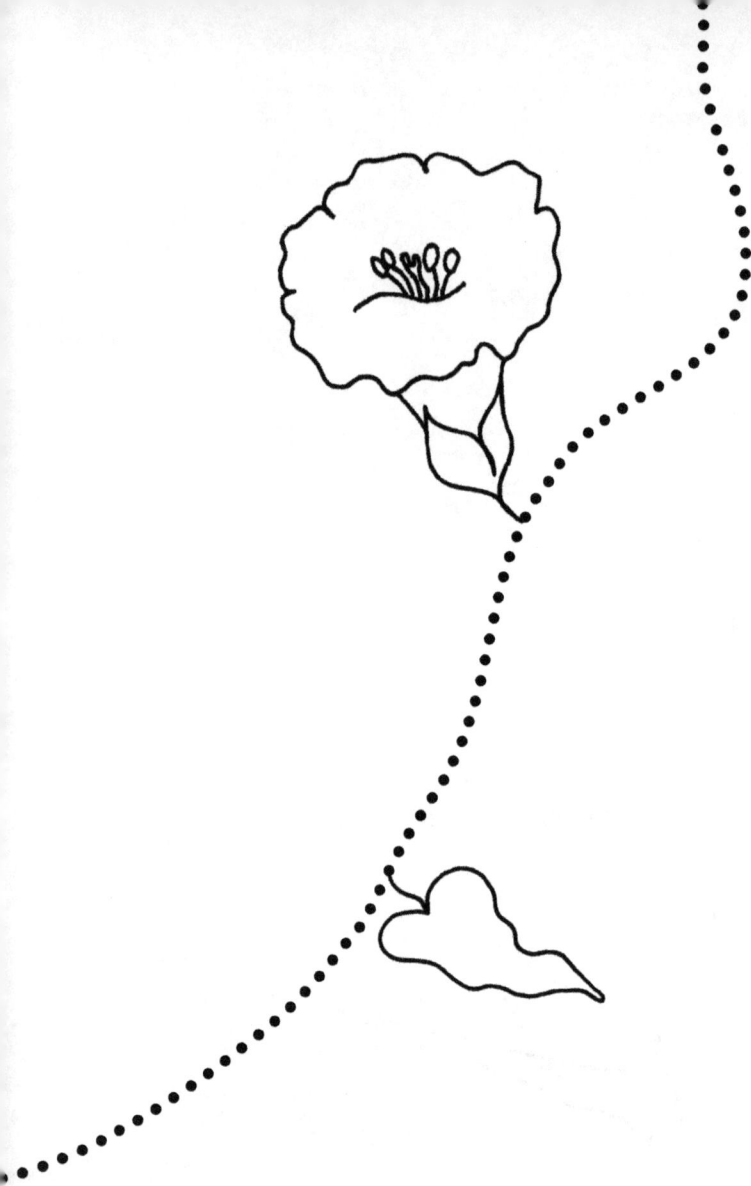

Table of Contents

III

I

as a child she burned

her hand picking up a stick of glowing
metal from a bonfire out amongst shells

not shells like those found on a beach with
a pale luminescence being grown for protection
by soft unboned creatures to save them
from the many predators of the deep, but

shells of bombed out buildings after the war
that started just before
she existed, and she carried the scar of it

said that she could smell her skin, her flesh
burning before she dropped the almost molten
poker, or whatever it was that had somehow got in
-side the flames, soaked up all that heat, and must
have seemed—glowing as it did from orange to red
then a brilliant white, to be alive itself, to be

hot with a life

it was emitting, and she'd caught it
within the innocent grasp at light she'd made

she showed the scar sometimes—a faded
location on the map of her skin—the way

the memory never did

thought says it burns now that light, that heat

II

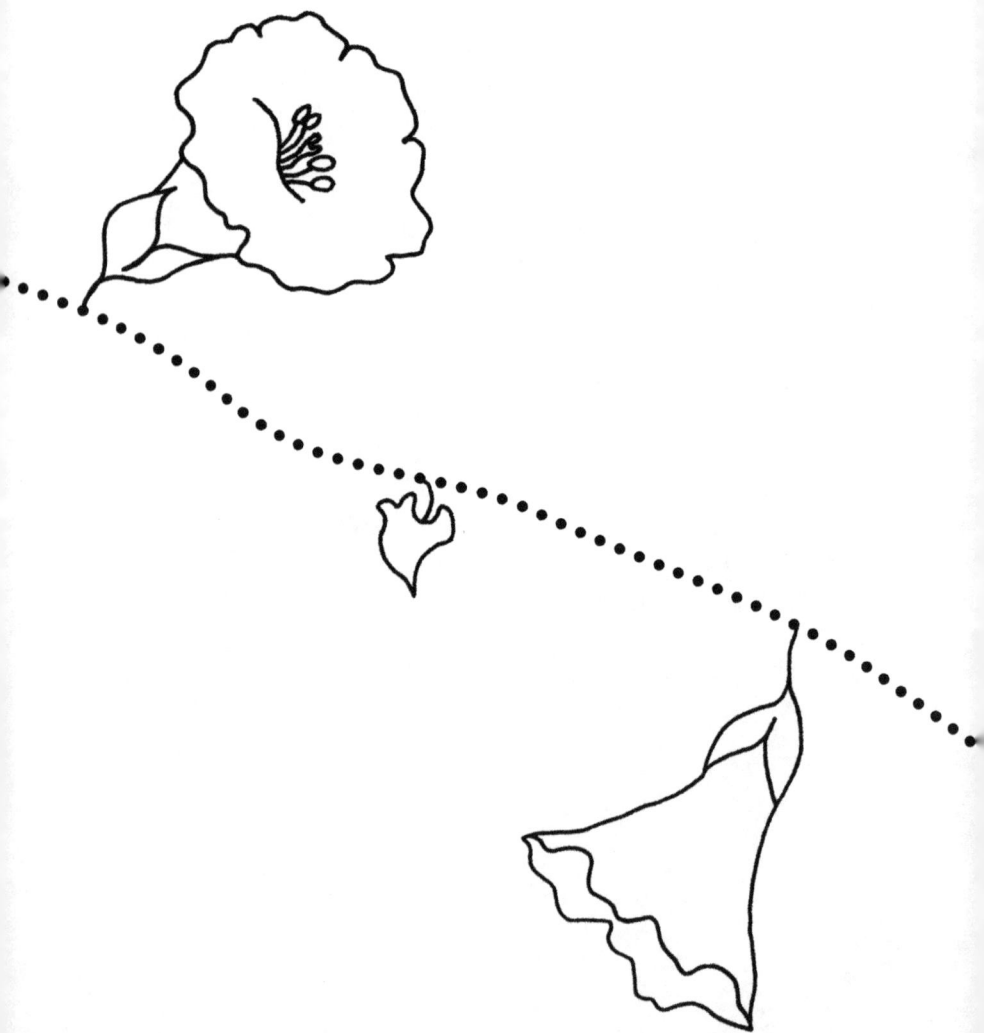

Bindweed

(after Margot)

a twine knots through the raspberries
pulls the long straight stems together
erasing what paths between the canes
had been left for us to enter when
the blood clot fruit was ready
the only way in is to pull
long strands of the bind weed clear

breaking a siege happening over years

all across the allotment phosphorescent
white flowers ghost from no-where
she called faerie hats when she was little
nothing can be done except to remove each one

The roots when they come are strangely fat
smooth and white like amoebic worms

What there is it takes and uses.

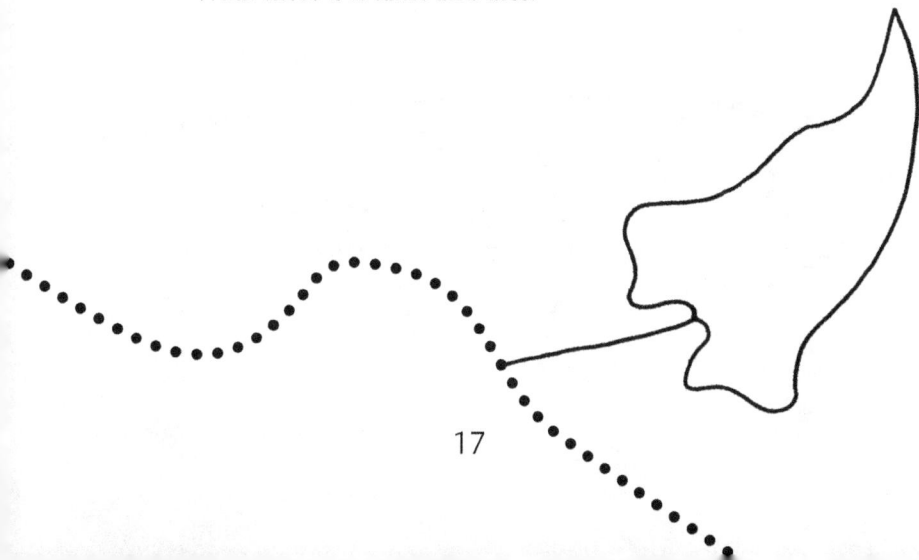

Passing thought

Reality went past in a large white van
as I walked to work this morning

I couldn't see through the mirrored glass
still wouldn't recognise it.

It must be heavy though
to need a van to carry it about

certainly wouldn't want it to hit me

Tomorrow there might be a future
being taken south in a trailer, or perhaps

a universe slowly passing in a hearse

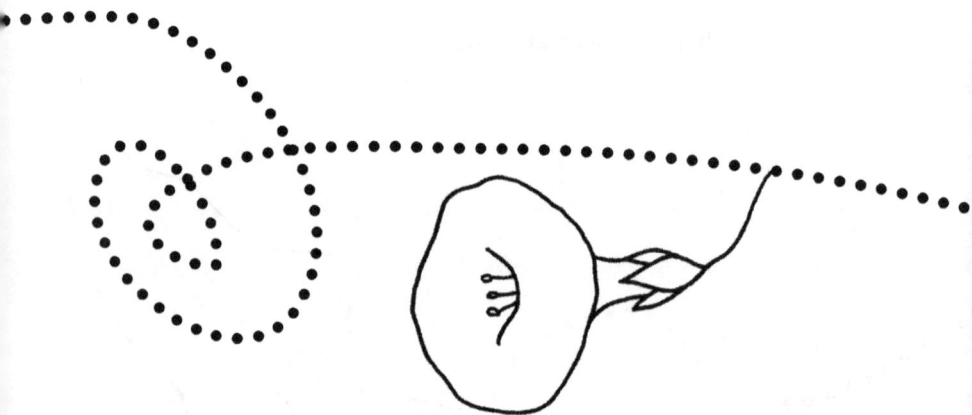

where i was placed in the driving seat of a dumper truck aged three

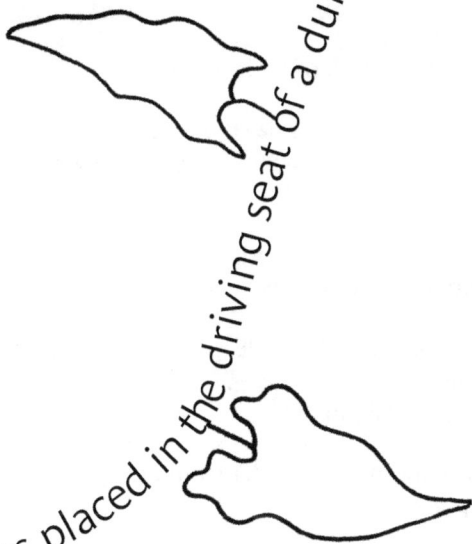

there are dreams of salting

vegetables laid out in trays

like those collections of animals
found in the drawers of a museum
each sleeping above
some coded invocation of Latin

the salt used a rough irregular grain so sharp to the touch it bites in
to the flesh of the hand chosen to scatter it
like witch hazel once stung a grazed knee—the remedy
infinitely worse than the ailment

miners swung
a pick at the solid wall
sweat pooling at the back of their necks
to a reservoir that breaks
every time they stretch and raise the long
handled blade for another swing that judders every
single bone of their body

others follow whose job is to gather
every fragment of salt that falls

scoop grit and rocks into heavy leather baskets that they pass
back along the seam
raise up on ropes and pulleys

to meet a soft light miners are deprived of
and be transported

'Africa, I

want to go to Africa' she says

I think of the cost,

the time, and images
of poverty and dust

rise up. A barren land,
dying elephants, tents swarming like flies,
thin, thin people, guns, hear children's cries.

She wants her brother.

Others

i don't know but it could well be that there has always been an awkwardness
others tell me sometimes but this does not tally with the scenes in my head
perhaps this is how it is for everything I feel that there is an inside and outside
we are not just flesh and cannot be found within a ribbed carcass
or behind the soft plastered brick of a house all florid colours
wallpaper and carpets—it is something else—if an actor
i am become unable to work the muscles of this face, or fully
inhabit this body, the part, or bring a complete understanding of the
character with all its weaknesses and frailties—as if a puppet
had loosed its strings and still not fully got used to the feeling
and this must be the same for everyone—although I recall
lifting my daughter and placing her child's face to my cheek—some
of her warmth moving from soft skin to older whiskery
skin—an infusion that seemed all the charge hope energy
of a young heartbeat—and remembered when i was happy and
everyone i met responded with a smile—smiles have a habit
of travelling swiftly face to face—they do not change as
words do into Chinese whispers of the playground—they say
just what they say—even if the source or reason behind it changes

i wonder if Chaplin, expert at conjuring laughs and tears could inhabit
fully his own skin—or if his brother Syd understood him—or his sad mother
or if he was searching through each film—the tramp—to live as this other

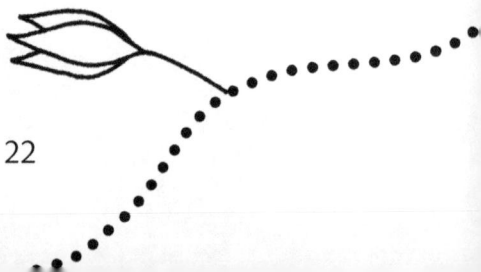

from . . . Blackness library
and other inconsequential things.

Nineteenhundredandten
on the glass
drinks to think before
immediacies
cut stone

more willow than flint his small frame
dances a cane so that it ticks along
as light as shadow on a sundial
his flat cap never a hat might
have floated into Cattle Market Tavern
on Cross Lane to stand by these men

or been shoulder to shoulder with them
at Salford Labour exchange, touched
as the injuries of the days injure his

hereandnow . . .

this 'edging to the goods' is all
turning to be, or not be, pinioned
on the crossbeam of days join
where the light pools in
and good shadow falls to summon
'intent'. breathe in
inheritance awaits habitation
or more precisely, a dwelling place

in fragmentia—

inside there are
blooms in the back parlour
spun of tender vibrations

        day was wet clay and noise until men
        abandoned the cement mixers, dumper trucks,
        and diggers to us who played on them
        after hours, when each was a bright splinter
        blossoming at the tree-lined street corner
        on a plot of waste land where fires lit
        night flowers against a darkening sky. Spitting
        stars of sputters eased us of the terrors
        waiting, always waiting, out there

an eye-star
or the first bright dot on a line
begins a murmur of harmonies
link of sounds

        needling together strands of wool unballing
        themselves a loosed skin against his
        own that will be a winters itch once all
        the seams are joined. to be grown
        into and pulled-more-giving, to be passed
        on. 'You will wear' was clicking from
        the high backed chair where a fear of colours,
        glorious and outlandish, to die defending, must be faced.

codifications of the land here
in absence requires a line
of flight capable of the—

bottled up, and still
within each cell
small feet step
quadrangles

alone in a signal box sweats
the night shift as the Luftwaffe
overhead bomb other targets

exposed blooms light blackness
as rails shift to split the rolling stock
a hopeless chaos of sweats pulled

slips from the palms of his hands

hallucination and dread sit quiet
on the edge of a bed at the far end

as unstable and unfriendly
as the quarry walls
are innocent

catching and threading and twisting and turning
hand and eye occupied there is no time
to think, dwell on shocked things, and this
is therapy, standing knee high
to a child—a walnut stained box-wood frame.
the wicker stool whispers of a course of days
at the sanatorium. the 'piano stool with tray'
that claimed all the heavinesses of this man

a child skips
a smile skips
sparrowlike
sweet as condensedmilk

we skate on a surface of shadows

too fast, really too fast, to be aware
of, for example, the studied stillness of trees or
the parasitical tenaciousness of moth desire
—such a great distance only to fuck and be extinguished—
whose time whittled multifaced eyes formed for movement are
so filled up with light that they miss,
always, the warm full womb of darkness.
                                        There is
no separation between things—the states
we observe are only that—states
whose borders we set as our studies,
and this brief, too brief, flame
consumes us as it consumes them.
No reason exists except that we make
the same way—whittling slowly from time,
the imperfect reflections of memory and feeling
always occluded by that thing desire
—the only guides those fools pleasure
                                        and pain.
There is little reason—we skate on a surface of shadows
and only live each day's sunshine
                        each day's rain.

where i learnt a taught history and about other countries.

Last of light reclines on blue

bean bags by the Tiber drinking, talking, listening.
I dreamt of war last night,
                    don't know why. It
was. It has happened before.
                           Disturbs.

The band plays
                    'we don't need no edukation',

as the Franco Angeli exhibition calls back to Vietnam—
to the boat that he was shot at in
from both banks of the river. Fear
alive in his voice as he explains that they might die
leaving their only child alone in the predatory world.

There is spring water runs under San Clemente
though it is only apparent where gushes sound
at the very deepest level of the excavations, it cools
the walls and air so that the 1st century small
abode that is the earliest dwelling found under there
is the most agreeable to walk through. Chuckles
of water being close are a tenuous hope
to be out-side of the chill of this enclosed stone
no light could penetrate, where shade is
all encompassing, all powerful, and every step is
weighed carefully. Above us a fresco, and a line
of script, that the guide tells us, is an ancient language

changing in form to the modern. Translated it says,
'come on you son's of bitches, pull'.

Quantas QF068 22:50 Flight to Perth

(watching BEASTS OF THE SOUTHERN WILD)

Overlord of the dry-World -I
suspended in aluminium

am occupant of a tub fed by hidden
springs   Below the Buffet

earth is moving   We batter
through air plugged in

to whatever it is we plug into.
Sometimes things leak and can no longer

be fitted back together.   When some
me is lost get a drink.
                              Salute!

The Indian Ocean is a feast
of moaning catfish.   A wild pig

of a storm runs all wet
bristles and pointing tusks.

The bus from Scarborough beach

They took the front seats the only
'originals' we encountered. And one
casually looking in at everyone else on the bus asked
'what colour are you? what colour are you?'
Peering at the faces of those close by
who ignored her, stone, looking away
embarrassed perhaps at the question
directed at them.   The worse

for drink, or loosened up
depending on your point of view
the rest of them, three or four
quietly waited for journey's end.

Half hoping something would happen
thought said 'if she asked me the question
I would say I was red'—just to see her reaction.

They all got off at the edge of the town

Lullaby

Nights of hearing
cars pass in the black,
radios playing what
may be some thing
recognisable, or not—
nights of hot stillness
become seamlessly this
shush of rain being
sussurations pooled skin,
unravelling in ways
open door faces
where just a fallen hair is
weight unbearable,
milling the air

Cuba

She names the fruit she gives me
that is strange to me
and writes the name in my book.

A Zapote as big as a pear.

It has fired brick skin and crinkly hair.
Within is a pinkish-red succulent
flesh, and a stone bigger than a Quails egg,
smaller than a Hens, that is
shiny, brown and white. When I bite
the ripe flesh is sweet and wet.

In the waiting room

ones with the proper paperwork who had
quietly answered all of the usual proof
of identities whispered across the desk
were now seated uncomfortably on a bendy
plastic chair catching at names released

to the air as a summons to one of the
strange

mouthy doors as a man nudges
his neighbour and slyly opens a cupped

hand to reveal

embedded deep—a thick nail
stake in meaty flesh that bleeds

Sydney—Art

After the giant concrete light bulb,
is the sound of water trickling,
the door where fear and damp is,
photographs of people asleep in doorways,
a naked man and a naked woman turning over and over on the floor.
A heavyset bronze man gives another smaller man a piggyback,
and an aged wrinkled man reclines on a deckchair. (He)
is naked and has a woman's sex.

There are dresses fixed upright with barbed wire heads
and open-book heads. There are films
of beach-huts dancing, people reading spread newspapers, cattle
taking showers.

A whirligig has wooden bats in waistcoats hanging from it . . .

We walk through. Or stop to read notices that tell us
something of what we are seeing . . .

We do not touch those things we are
told we must not touch. I would
bring all these things together
in different ways, showing

the apes are not the centre.
There is something more important happening,
something that has been missed.

the red of the leaves

of the tree that stands in the corner of the car park opposite
the office, would everyday flame—
warming me
even across the small distance and beyond
the high wall of long lane

no other tree was near it

a wild thing beyond any design the roots breaking
the bird glooped tarmac about it
its seed obscuring windscreens being
carried by the wind as a sort of grit
that fit itself into the tread of shoes to be dispersed wherever—

the red of those leaves coloured
each day as if the boughs were a frame for a sea

each leaf a herald of change
a blood remembrance of others

in some lights the whole tree seemed to be melting
and though it stood firm, it wavered, as if
just at this particular place time alternated
and it was both present and absent

was witness to something fleeting

a messenger

Recipe

this one needs the full
yellow sun of a day old egg
to bind the sticky that is spread
out flat on the fine white
sand-web made of a wild sea shore—

the warm sea's coming in bubbles waft
to a ribbon twists in the froth
and spumes alive

in tides that should be gathered
together using an old iron pan and colander

so the salt water drains and every
small creature caught to its starchy
fingers—sea snails with shells like flugelhorns
or tiny white translucent crabs that scuttle
sideways and are stops and starts
like wary mice—must be carefully placed
back amongst the waves to float away

like words do

tree rests

an arm along the top of the low stone
wall letting it take all
of the weight of the long journey it made

from seed to this—gargantua
of many sworled faces that peer

there is a crushed nose, a cauliflower ear
a bruised eye, a mouth punched closed
with a fat-mastic tongue

age has picked at the flesh of it
loped a limb or two
so that now it might not do all it wanted to

when it rushed out green missives to the far
and the bird nests were plentiful

where what was Spring, Summer, Autumn, Winter, is no longer

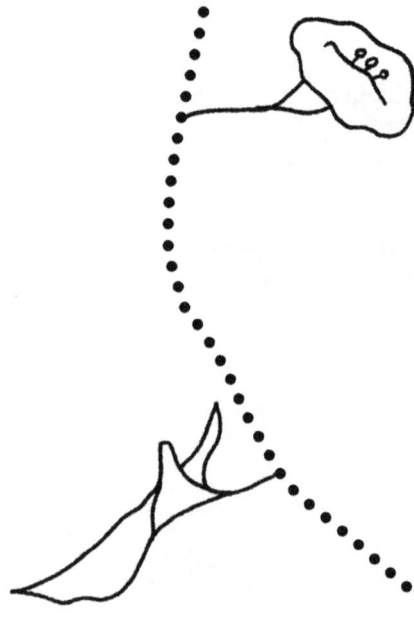

the island

the snub nose of the cathedral's
large stained glass window of flying
saints and peasants, with at its centre
a man staked out on a cross, resembles
most one of those Chinese dragons that look
like small long haired dogs made fierce—
a Pekinese perhaps . . .
armoured as for mortal combat
two front paws lined up exactly
symmetrical to its blunt nose
eyebrows are gargoyles bushing out each side
to spit fire and oil far and wide
while the whole chamber of the body lies
all entrances and exits
the other side of high iron railings
taking the entire length of the green

is coated in a rigidly pleated lead
awkward knees sticking out a perpendicular
crudely bring up the rear

a myth of first

stand or fall
there could be no rest
light and darkness all
is axis all connects

and from the eye a Sparrowhawk
flew up and high and higher still
till a shaft of yellow scanned about
the tangling black to where trees grew
strange night flowers unfurling soft
fruit and a fall
of bat awaked from hollow boles
codes sex to plants that trap loosed light
to set an edge as everything
touched bled

lost without colour was Sparrowhawk

and out from roots dug deep
spread arms turned branches weeping
hair tangled stars that fixed
leaves soaking brilliance

and colours danced to bring
happenings of chance again

Merlin soared weaving

a canopy of yellow and green
and shielded from stars hot rays
blackness birthed first day

The Blue Mountains

train at Central Station
goes to Katoomba. We pass
Gallipoli Mosque, a Turkish
Welfare Association, the Granville
Hotel, a tunnel where
Spice of Sky is written high
across the walls, The Sari
Eclipse at 60 Station Street.
At Parramatta the platform opposite
is empty except for three automatic
food dispensors. Hungry
Jacks Palm Trees. Hunter
Eye Laser car-parks full.
Rolling lawns are parks.
Flats are for sale. Next stop
Westmead and hospitals,
a university campus. Doors
close, 'please stand clear'.
We go by the emergency help
-point, through the steep
embankment, and the tall rises
and visitor parking spaces.
More palm trees. Bungalows
all have large satellite dishes.
Under bridges. On to Blacktown
and Mr Pings eatery where doors open
but no-one leaves, no one
gets on. At Penrith a dilapidated
building is the Museum of Fire having
white paint flaking from its walls.
Emu Plains and half way to sleep;
to Blaxland, Warrimoo, Valley Heights.
Miss a few to Katoomba then walk
to Echo Point and Three Sisters where

the seed husks in the trees are dry
tongues pointing up to the sky

Waking to Opua, the sand

is sand and small stones like flints and broken shells and unwinding
green pods that the Mangroves are from, and those
sea-weeds whose feet curl about rocks to hold to
and whose heads hide amongst many ribbon-like tresses
going in every direction that have come loose
and drifted here

He does not know it but we are following the small square
shouldered man wearing a wide white brimmed hat

Is the wet
sand more easy to walk on than the dry because of the water
held in it? Are we walking on water?

Tidelines of green seedpods, some split
into four thick leaves grow out
a thick root to grasp something heavy and fixed to anchor
A steady in the coming

We pass Te Rangi Cross to be under a canopy of bright
blue flowering Bindweed, and high Fern

We descend again passing a closely mown lawn and sprawling
fig tree heavy in fruit ripening from pale red to purple tainted
sweet things. The dead leaves

of some ferns hang like dry ropes
at the seas edge, and fingers of Mangrove show
where the tide breaks

Moss is a soft felt we slip on, taking
the path up-hill and about
to the cove where a raised wooden platform of slats
have a wire netting fixed on to grip

The platform ends at an old Pine tree rising
out of the soft bed of its own shed
needles where we rest and a fly
buzzes at my toes

At Opua are black butterflies and
the familiar smells of wood

Where

the hairy headed cumulonimbus
gradually grows a limb, it stretches
from a pocket to a pocket

of trees threaded through large droplets;
rain—its hungry lips
leave expectant ponds where Geese

could break flight to rest on the long
journey to Africa;
a waistcoat of scattered light—

thrown in a flash of temper
is found suffocating,
and taken off, a quick release.

The tarmac's glisten bounces accidents
of headstands, cartwheels, and backflips
that run as slick as rain off a water-dogs back,

as the low growl of a cloud-splitter
sounds attack too late
for whatever has missed the straight

and narrow tongue is swallowed
whole by the impenetrable black
on either side—the only way to pass

from the wild to the stone-bridge,
and over to where the lights of the city
are usually, but on this day's night

they hold fast witness to what power, what force—
shakes the long established

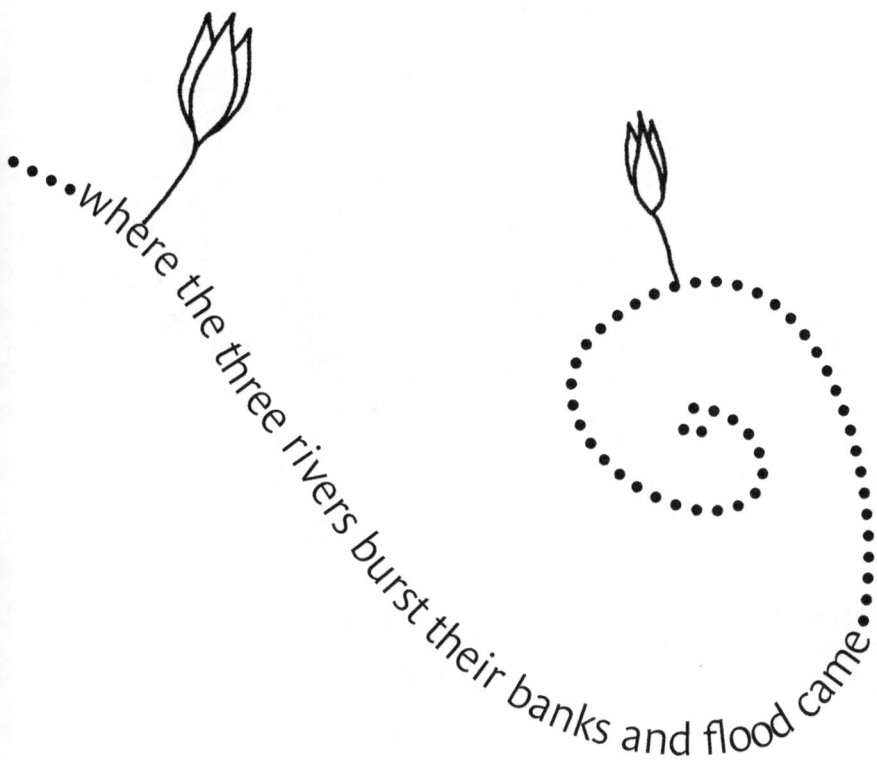

where the three rivers burst their banks and flood came

Old woman Heron

drank her own
reflection, stood off
the stilled outer of
the river where
mud and sand slipped
slowly together
to a full body. She

waded deep into the still
moving down-river, until
leaving water she disappeared
into scrubland where

a hieroglyph waiting
could no longer read her.

Berlin

reclines in the big hall
where the roof is all arches and domes
like myriad bowls upturned

reconstructed on columns of herself.

The lights of her eyes are melts
of snow on mountains
where skies are fields of blue.

She gazes at nothing
hunches forward shouldering
all the old Gods and Myths—the air
is too warm and her arms hang loosely
for she has resigned her whole being
saying 'get it over'.

A loose sweep of black
is her blouse off one shoulder
and the whole drowse of her

catches at the red
flower in her hair.

where Penny showed me all the way to the tops of her multi-coloured tights

Over the water

Someone alone
crossing the stone
bridge in heavy
rain speaks to me

No protection
or help with the heavy
cotton bag that seemed
to shrink on straps

that ran across
her shoulders as
she fought her way
looking down
at the ground tunnelling
her head out
the wind onrushing

a way behind
had just climbed
nineteen stone steps
to emerge where sky was
made of large white
colanders shaking
drops that soaked us
in an instant

Wild things are
all quiet knowing
hid safe

Ignoring what was
plain before us
we carried on
to the riot of a storm

a desolate message

rose like a loaf in the bread of my blood
glob sweetened with the fruit of childhood

an end of childhood—all
loose folded, richly heady

it closed with 'take care, with love'
and i was spurred to seek news

and failing in this placed the page
carefully back inside the desk

beside the photograph of stone
only for it to rise again

lighting confusions
melting under the skin

reaching out to cross the seas
a taste of pain

pale Hedgehog

beyond reflection on the glass
something stirred, something approached us.

unrecognised at first in the confusion
of dining table, chairs, and us in the room

it came as if pulled on a string
ever closer—following

a scent it snuffled on the path from
when wild edge taking form was common.

if an upturned boat—it had
a hull of spines and a dainty leg set
at each round corner—dancing it
roughly on the water, until the prow nose
lost what it was drew it near to us—
and stopping, it looked weakly all about
in the closing of the light
unknowing what strange joy it was
to us who'd watched this other approach
that thought had tricked into the visitation
of a rarely absent loved one

At the Mall, Beijing she is

emptying her late teens
in the World of the upright freezer

of plastic bags of different pastry-shapes
at the Paris Baguette, Wangfangju shopping district.

She wears the universal white chefs hat
she pushes back, and a spotless white
apron, blue jeans, and those very soft
canvas trainers that are now in fashion
and the white cotton gloves she pulls on

for protection against the cold
bags she pulls out and drops
one
       by
             one
onto different coloured plastic trays.

She stands face flushed
one leg a pivot
she can swing about on
working quickly.

Across the plaza in 'Signora'
all the assistants wear
the same grey dress with horizontal black bars
as the dummy in the shop window.

One of them stops and stares
at a young woman loudly
telling her boyfriend to buy
some-thing that he can not find.

Exasperated she throws her hands to the air
absolutely sure she can speak

what-ever it is she wants into existence

The hollow

in the road passes the site of the Leper hospital
as indicated by a sign in a blue circle.

Everything today is slow as if under water.
Undergrowth has overgrown.

No part of this was sown.
Bushes straggle into trees

trees reach up for air.
The Alsatians that are always caged, bark

desperately. Wild flowers having no name
flame here.

Birds flit bush to tree
pulling good dark in

about themselves to fit
finding what reason they have

to be a part of this
              wild

long abandoned place.

where i would gather buckets full of frogs, newts, and toads, and put them back

At the Museum of Modern Art, Tokyo, Japan,

the pitch showroom shininess hit
the exact pitch my inner
ear could detect
becoming this thought that softly coalesced
connecting the shock of the newness
of temples built of meccano
and reassembled every seven years;
of skyscrapers; of only seeing
showroom-ready cars;
the finished straight-edged pristine look of everything

to this womb of paintings of a war
when our two countries were enemies
I am hush quiet, everyone is

seeing 'Compatriates in Saipan Island remain faithful to the end'
the horrors; women screaming
arms upraised; children looking
out from behind guns;
malnourished men shooting weapons
as they cling to the bare rock that is the island

The 'signpost to Hades'
is a frieze of charcoal and black
is the ends of socks, the odd shoe, an odd
boot sticking up makes a road
of what remains
after everything is burnt away
in a conflagration unexplained
whatever was closest to
the earth is char.

I make notes about another
a shadow overlapping a shadow
and an attendant whispers
to request that I write in pencil, not ink She insists
on giving me a small pencil to note
the transience of things   I am

a photograph of an open wound
being sewn.

there are desolate landscapes

                                 and a child
alone in a long bare corridor cries
as she turns away from a burning light

There is a patient receiving visitors
a babe in its mothers arms
and paintings of misformed creatures that are
women bathing who lose their limbs
and men that are soon nothing
more than torsos
Soon brash colour demonstrates against
whatever it is that the police arrest
people for demonstrating against
                            there are masses marching
                                   Steel girders
jut through the outer skins
of buildings melting away
being peeled back
And another woman is so slight that her struggle to move the large
bag of stones up the steep steps that go on and on
into the far distance must surely fail

                              There are
women in traditional dress
a row of urinals
                         a skull aims a rifle
daubs and smears and splatters chickens
drown in water, and a man
is covered in white feathers
as people soaked to the bone bend at the waist
while planting whatever it is
they must to survive

Strange designs of Onchi - tracings and scribblings—
somehow form a hand with fingers
held straight together and pointing thumb upward,
making liquid landscapes
visitors helplessly navigate One man
wears a black bowler hat A woman
covers her nose and mouth with a white cotton mask
Young couples are locked arm in arm,

                                                    unaffected,
as far as I see,
by the devastation that rolls
on through the gallery.

Perfect (old shoes)

Each one is worn to a tear
At the same point creased
A shell of moulded skin
Comfortably thin through wear
And treading lightly, with care, each pebble
Grit or pearl stone
Can be felt along the way
And though no longer watertight
They can feel the tightrope
Of each day
So while every walk's not perfect
Each one is

after Salford

was a corner council
house where they had
a garden—their first

later he told
of journeys back
and forth to Madams-

Wood collecting soil
so full of leaf mould—
it would never need

as children we ate
the Currants and Berries
Potatoes, Lettuces, Tomatoes and Grapes

made of the rustling
silence of that place
knowing nothing

except to be
what was light
being released

first they took the party

built by our fathers and mothers and their fathers and mothers
we found that the voices that should be ours
in the corridors of power—worked
only to make themselves millionaires

to do this they sold what had been carefully built
by our fathers and mothers and their fathers and mothers
that was owned by all of us
the hospitals and the schools
and cut all the branches of care from their roots
until what had grown over years bled

and they took, and took, and had

us fight a war that was not ours
shaming us

now we have other voices

where we protested and a good friend standing right beside me is arrested

The river rose

up in a massive wave which stopped
on end as if it froze.

All else stilled as if hit pause
could hold one moment from another—
could raise up even a river
busy plotting out its next excursion
to the shores beyond.

The river waited some obstruction
more than trees crossing in migration;
more than stone, iron, rust;
more than home, dust, loss;
more than kerbs by the canal
where burners burn to warm the hands,
the river waited something else
like a canvas waits the brush—
the deserted riverbed drying in front of
it—
the pebbles, stones, and grit
a flickering flame passed by
waited patiently aware no eye could split
the grey and white and blue and green
or take the sap out of the rain—

a river waiting untame

Skits.

leaf patina'd dusky earth
warm'd grey'd littered over with delicate crowns
of seed, twig debris, riffles of revealed
root, and uncropp'd grass straying
borderlessly to cow parsley, foxglove, nettle . . .
as the dapple shade air moves
green, moves all about, gently.

feathers become edges separated, billowed
about parts of the green leaf or blade angling
itself sufficient in the light.

water, chuckling plentiful water, runs
joins with more of itself running
all together over rocks, over building
waste, wooden frames, concrete blocks,
pebbles, and those smaller stones
that run to grains of sand and silt that run
to lodge in those places where green canopies break
down
to reflection, and are re-established below

the little weir
where jumping fish are.

ducklings follow mother
this stretch, and on another
a heron uncomfortably poses
unhappy on one leg
hungry head thrown back

stabbing beak skywards.

a shaft of black slants across each unblinking

eye. a butterfly, white in the yellow
buttercups and blue forget-me-nots
skits by a steel bench set in
what remains of a fire, the broken bits,

abandoned ash and char.

Skyway avenue has a first light of

established trees that reach over running down both sides of the long stretch,
between them flower beds, a radiant colour
of unnecessary drama,
where scared and sacred are brought together
in a wordless exchange
of people, who pass each other without ever touching.

The trees accommodate wood pigeons and collared doves
and are losing scabs of bark
in sobs
of reaction to the high lead in the atmosphere
close to the ground.
         There are
nervous dogs running around that form themselves into packs and scavenge
the litter bins, and backs of the restaurants
and takeaways that steadily look away
from all of this ruck, towards the sun rising in the early
mist of the new.

A man moves from under the awning of the old shabby
hotel striding purposefully from the grey
shade of one tree, to the next, and on.
A street-cleaner comes
pushing along a plastic bright yellow that he detaches a broom from
sweeps the paving with
empties, and replaces.

Gulls that had been fighting and craning
snapping their beaks at the rubbish and ripping in
-to yesterdays excess,
fly away as he advances.
A woman leans out of one of the high windows
of a hotel, and says that she doesn't know
why she keeps coming back here, pulls in

her head, disappears.
And a man's voice follows, says that she always tiptoes
when she's drunk. His words detach from the dark
to fall as if cast out and are gathered up with all
that enters the avenue unheeded.

Vans arrive and deliveries begin to to and fro
as if winching up the anchor of the day to go.

                                        Feeling it's tug and pull
on the concrete face of the street slowly filling. The grudging
resentment of the woman, now absent, and the distance
somehow remaining between all of the things
of this dumb show
that had waited for the light to be enough.

To be the exact equal to that that happened here,
taking off on this plane of cement and granite where neon
billboards flicker, selling through coffee starts that butter and crumb
the tin tables so hastily arranged, as the sun rises to open
every bud leaf and flower, turning them, and the ribbed cats lazing in warily,
into objects in a gallery of what might be
almost one day, or any other . . .

Skyway avenue has a first light of established trees
both sides of the long stretch . . .

Ox Eye Daisies.

a foot fumble through liquescent-apparancies
the green-way perspires

one element slides through another,
crossing sodden-pasture

bog-rutted cow-patted, missing
small clearances,
a path known as a child.

The break in the barbed wire is mended.
The slope where the Ferns are,

                                        above the Reeds

would pull and peel back a slither
to fire at each other like arrows,

sucks our feet.

Young grasses we heard
whatever wind said,

pliantly made
our branches home
to birds and insects,

found suns in the field
dressed in white robes
that opened wherever sky touched

We climbed ladders of stems
taken away, and would pull them
out from the socket earth

to make them into chains

hunger's

open note of sky
                           stretching
changes the troubled sea of itself
wrinkles as it edges
catches and releases
a seam of things
                           continuing
where there are voices in the air
rising like the smoke of a fire
that clings to the woollen fibres
                                          it flavours
with that taste that fire
                    makes
the outside blowing
the memory of heat
into heat
through the heights
of itself
        sparks
seeding the air
with familiar things
a forked tree
standing at a lonely roadside junction
waiting on the particular—
some dirty bricks are
walls rearranging themselves
of factories
outside of any volition
momentarily as they were
when we were hungrily
running together
staring down black
                    melting tongues of tarmac

sucking our soles
each step a disengagement
            made up after
so longingly that only the eye's different
searching for
innocence as if it could be out there still
turning the corner
miraculously whole
                    a raggedy white

We talked,

only that, talked
about the other night, who was there,
what was said, all those sort of inconsequential
things.
She asked me if I remembered her
telling me before
that she was transforming, transforming
I asked what did she mean?
Like a butterfly? like a chrysalis perhaps?
A chrysalis, yes, she replied, something like that.
And what would she be at the end of it?
what was happening inside?
A realignment of the planets
becoming seeds that feed on light,
an opening up
so that what was hiding before might grow,
and never stop

on the mottled trunk

of a tree—it disappears

is only apparent as edges
animated by currents
of scurrying air

moving across the plain
face the World is
making rootlessness

the idea and the thing—this
fragile addict follower
of a chemical laden air

the notion of a deity
forgotten, or super-ceded
by one more deadly

poison to whatever—what intricacy
its being here, and not
hiding entirely in another's language

She says that she doesn't mind it.

That it's their country
That if they want to know what we do, and whether
we know anyone who lives there
and a part of our medical history, that's ok
with her. It rankles with me.

I am landlocked in stares
anchored in ice flows.

All this is noise, nothing more.
Waves are stretching
that were not visible before.

When the time comes I will tip out my pockets
take off these worn shoes, and follow.

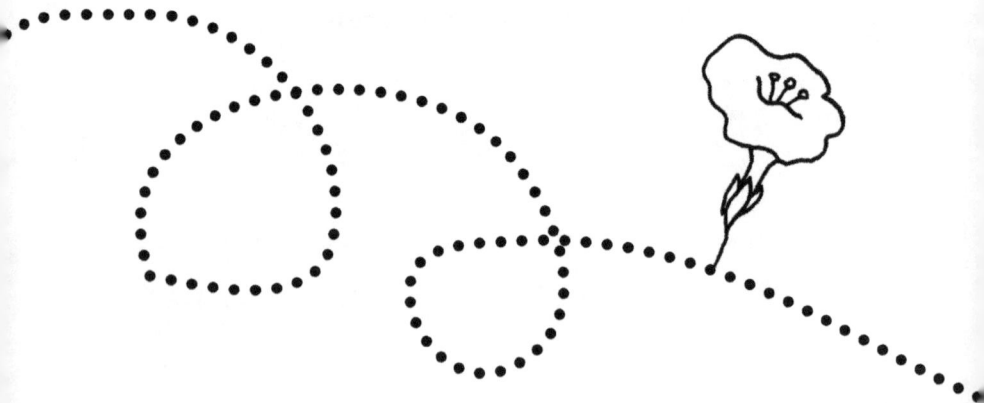

Inside the Asahi Brewery Headquarters

a curvaceous bronze
labelled 'reclining nude'
lies on her side—
body raised up on the jack
of one arm making
a triangle—her impassive flat
planed oval face looks down
her body to the free
hand resting on the curve

of hip   The building
is a gold reflective block
with a strange gold horn projecting
from it—K says
is a drop at rest on the top of a huge
black plinth—that is also a building

where power put businessmen in charge of our children's schools

A sign in the Museum of Modern Art

tells that 'the education corner is disinfected eight times a day'.

'Root' is a bronze
naked man standing on a tree
trunk that appears
to have roots at each end

the trunk must be
a large cross-section of root
branchlings to small roots
at each end—the man

stands on the thick mid-section staring
down at the rootlings

of night's dream—a black

man is writing a Symphony
of the torments he hears

when he transcribes a black girls life

the children of America take off
their shoes and socks in the playground
until the World is become large

piles of shoes that have barefoot
children sitting proudly astride them

Tree Creeper nimbles up

as if part of the tree has
returned after having studied
the lives of beetles and insects—
to fight such threats, jabbing
into crevices and cracks in the thick
rind the tree makes

of years. One with the tree, it
is a stand against gravity
held perpendicular in light air

plays astronaut effortlessly
dancing feet up-anchoring
weightless, long-toes gripping

tight to bole, a furried activity
it stabs critically at every strange
life it uncovers. Feeding

fulfils a bargain struck
before it was born
to glean whatever—

skitting about the centre
reading the map the cover the book of it
then to forget, to forget

be a usual part of the landscape dealing
out healing death

the hesitation

is a Japanese garden
beyond the small waterfall where gently tended trees
bend into themselves as if to absorb
great age, stoop—a path
winds to a house of rice paper
where walls throw shadows that tell
of tenants who adopt a stance
of humility, and within this stilled
space there is that kind of silence, or hush, of important
things presumed to be thought of—it is
as if the space is a clearing
a foreshadowing of knowledge—the air
somehow edging to a future
it tries to latch on.

Drips.

The taps dripping numbers fluently
There must be a sink full by now
Or would be if the plug were in.

We could collect them randomly
Making patterns like ice crystals
Each one unique. We could calculate

Probabilities, bet on the next drips
Identity, rank them by the swell
Exhibited before they fall.

They are squeezed out whole.
There are no fractions of a drop,
No halves or quarters,

Each is complete. Listen
To their sound, that was ten.
The musical notation for each note

Would resemble them, a drop
Black on the stave. Is the sound
In proportion to the density

Diameter and weight?
I wish it would stop.

as unlikely as just one.

at the far end of the lawn
a feeding supermassive black hole
has adopted the familiar shape
of a small, gentle, timid looking
rabbit grazing on the grass and nettle,
dock, and buttercup
grown up while we were away
that spray their offspring to remote colonies
displacing weaker grass that we hoped for
drilling themselves in, and mining the rich
minerals they discovered and tapped into,
so that all air will be a profligate seed super-highway
as quickly as possible transporting green wherever
serendipitous winds, and even the gulf stream might
inadvertently direct them, so that the whole circular
process of channelling water and carbon and everything
that is powered by the light of our nearest distant sun
through what we term living things, continues
to happen on this small, partly green, and mostly blue
planet in this particular solar system of this universe
of the probable many universes out there, and beyond
where feeding supermassive black holes are also disguised
as rabbits tearing up and chewing on what tender grass
remains of what used to be a carefully manicured lawn

ennui, with houseboats . . .

is a walk in such a small place
that history castled and cathedraled
plotted out three rivers running
to run together so that
soon enough the same imposes
like this—grey, misty, shoeless

trees the frost will obliterate
the shoots of that push of the hard burning
back—but after all
come or not it's one and the same.
The weather mountain shifts one foot
to the other, and we are too slow
too encumbered to escape. birds fly,

metamorphoses. Some things,
it seems, never change, though spirits lift

with the Sun. I heard a piano play,
the one we gave away long years ago
I would jiggle the keys of passing
—thinking how mathematics and music are
locked together

thinking in eights.

In a kind of a dream state
you can enter thought drifts
from where things are
solid and stable, to another
sand running (so to speak) underfoot,

tides rush. What is it that scrambles
everything so that something must
happen, (a bell ringing
is the classic), a slap might,

brings things back.

There was a time the last
of the tribe told
fireside stories of itself and of the big
outside. it was in, as tight

as a drums seeds would bounce off of
sounding rhythms speaking days

into being
to people them.

A dream? Some dark
madness? After all

we took the ferry
to Sausalito to see the gaily
painted houseboats

walking beside the River, until eventually
we turned about, not quite getting there.

Madrid

oh how unhappy you are!

Early to the airport train
and some poor sod's been overnighting
in the concrete underpass where
mosaics of the Border Reivers are.
There is a pink pillow, and scattered
plastic cups

—the train is
a line of blue carriages with shocking pink doors,
a kind of loose wave designed series of lines traversing
the lower parts. The guard
waves—and starts

us high till dark grows
leaf and tuft
through the cloud flow, and the few
lights emerging
from the centre are molten lava.
Trees are a crusted coral flower opening
from inside, giving
an orange pink light.

What were bomblets are rust buds

the moving sea displaces,
and loud shudders through us
feeding the ponytail of the girl who moves her head
to the aperture
air pours through.

Dry as a Ravens feather,
dry as grass holding the colour of the sun
growing on the sleepers of the railway line where trains no longer

run.

Talk is of leaving
the recognised order of things.

Madrid, Madrid,

is frozen inside the stilled Palacio of glass in Retiro
where a child's swing is fixed at an angle of forty five
by a series of lines
that attach it to the base of an old Bontempi
from when vinyl was
as black as rubber soles
that stuck us to the melting tar roads of summer.

My man San Fran had dropped a line
in the form of a drop-handled motorbike with alloy wheels and wires
with fluttering flags, and such, that was all shine—

And Jim sings in my ear 'well we're
on our way, and we can't go back'. I would

the river was full.
Elsewhere
is a shipwreck of such mute colour
that the Bowler-hatted man wearing
a long grey coat, carefully
places his hands deep in
-side the pockets.
Outside the PCE,
and others are marching,
chanting, and whistling for simple human dignity

all the way to the Gran Via, and further.
And I am
a visitor returned
who had hoped to get away
from the breaking apart of things,
the fracturing of the seasons,
ever rising seas.
If only for a moment in 'Madrid, Madrid, Madrid, Madrid',
as the Edwin I remember said it.

And though I have never undertaken or engaged in recreational
waterboarding all hope is passing
the lines of armoured wagons, the dogs
held tight to the leash, and the police vans

and I am drowning slowly regarding Picasso's 'Harvesters'. Two oxen,
with working people carefully worked in oils,

—how he captured them with such precision!
who are lifting hay onto a waiting wagon on a gloriously yellow day
so bright it reminds of the flowers on the Gorse that shine
like tears. We are born children

to a thirsty sun, human-animal beings innocent before iron
and machines set about us,

here on the beach paddling to the sea, and again

in 'the Garden of Eden'
where the chosen animals have gathered, predators
and those preyed upon,
to a circle of light in a clearing
as Adam and Eve depart the day.

All of the wide avenues the marchers pass
gods of empire that look from high
classical fountains, to the flags, feet, heads, arms

that are Madrid Madrid Madrid.

What appeals is the easy way that beyond all of this green moves under
and around the bodies of four recumbent women—three of whom are
sleeping, or appear to be, and one
whose head is propped, who reads
from an open book.
And the way that almost all those that look
take an image of what they see
with a mobile phone, or camera. Storing it up.
Taking it away.

Another picture has blues and greens of water
swirl about the legs of two children
as though they are drinking.
And in the midst of the huddle of people photographing
a small woman displays
her wounded arm to her husband, who treats
the bleeding rash with ointment, and a plaster, before they retire
from the chatter of the tourists, to be alone
in the controlled and marshalled ranks of garden plants,
all clay pots of cut Geraniums,
to sit quietly on the cool
blue tiles there.

While suffocating locked inside Edward Hopper's
'Hotel Room'. (1931)
we become a woman in a one-piece bathing suit sitting alone
isolated from the World on a thin single bed,

reading a sheet
of paper laid flat across our knees
that anyone must take to be bad news.

A blue bowler-type of hat is,

worked with fabric flowers, or remnants, somehow found
and inexplicably placed atop of an old wooden dresser.
Away with its forgotten cares.
And laid flat
on the crudely painted floorboards are our two cases, or rather
a badly aged and battered leather case, and a sun
-faded fabric valise.
And beyond all of this
is the 'Bullfight' abstraction, is smearings

and smatterings,
mindless breakings apart and comings together.
In parenthesis
battle was lost when the river that was
the blood of the trees emptied and became
this bed of thorns.
Madrid
simply missed what was important. Mis-placed
what all freely possessed with sorely purchased chains
that even the singing Guadarrama winds
cannot undo.

New patterns spill from the tubes still—the tracks
move on randomly,

and applied tracings
slowly walk into a raging sea.

Waving salves of bathers, and (strangely) a pier,
arrive too late, I fear.
For Madrid
waits in the cloaca of the World
for a hard shell. It's soft
skin translating the Sun to a deepening,
a lesson of Time made by the living
that turns into sound, and moves
from a wild and contagious laughter,

to the 'scream of the Butterfly',
as Jim might say.

(Edwin—is Edwin Rolfe, Jim—is Jim Morrison)

Smothering

footlings of moss's.
Irregular brittle chains of lichen
from each finger nail.
Scuffled irregular scales.
All spun of nothing but water and air.
The muffled shocks of their being
disguised by time's slowing down
or speeding up. Whichever.
Seeing, the waves
affecting a shore of rods and cones,
unconcealing the maze that would
be all about us, She

wants Daisies. Ox eyes.
Clusters of bright yellow suns that sway
waist high, the summer. I

would trees, untamed,
feeling out the earth, needling
their way, hardened.
A reach of arms burdened with pur-
pose.

The simple live presence of the thing.

Car.

a coupé style car—do they call them?
boxy, with wings or fins
and set square headlights, chrome,
shiny wheels, a body
not painted so much to blush as to own—
there in the bashed in shed
with double doors and night

the wood frame damp and rotted

it made me uneasy, the car
of people i only vaguely knew . . .

Ice crystals sparked the Mackerel sky
as he said he was once so small, and the lobsters so big—
he could sit inside a shell—and row it

a naked woman clambers into a bath in the Kitchen bathroom

in 1936. A brown teapot
and a white teapot stand together with delicate cups
and saucers on a tray on a bench opposite
a white enamel sink. The white teapot is
lukewarm with stewed tea. There are
towels hanging from a high-line drawn across
the room separating the bath from the kitchen. These
were dampened with steam, and are dry now, and ready.
A middle aged bespectacled man stands before them
wearing a white shirt and white cotton trousers. He is
neither fat nor thin. He clutches
a pallet with one hand, and flourishes an artists brush
with the other. Another man stands
in front of him making notes in a black bound notebook. He
glances at the woman noting that she is not made properly
real, at the teapots that make him nostalgic for meals he once had
at a grandparent's as a child, at the sink that is not
the Belfast sink his wife used to want, and at the artist
who seems to be a sort of dandy, and is insignificant
in some vital way, to all of the happenings; the woman's bathing, the tea's
stewing away undrunk, the drying of the towels,
even the paint setting on the pallet
                 has more of life in it than he—

in the first dancing light
a white cloud gave a thumbs up

to Crows shadow puppet hands flapping
across a pale blue that is the colour you said
you wanted because for you it was the Med
with its long and perfect beaches of soft clean sand
sea that is warm and safe and so very salty
skin carries its taste licked by a smiling sun

while everything's begun give it up things say
desist in this controlling headstrong and wilful way
let the stones fall where they may let the tree
of man quiet down so that Crows stay their flights
of puppetry implacably on the branches to become
disquieting faces each with a meaningless expression

• • where waters rose so that we moved from Broad Street to the top of a hill • • •

When Crow makes that noise

feet planted, braced, square
on the ground neck and upper
primed, working
rhythmically sounding
the air, it is as if raw

vital life, unrestrainable

bursts through it from the very soil.

Lime trees have been sexing.

Sticky green seed scatter is a wind
attaches to the soles of shoes

a dream tarmac might have.

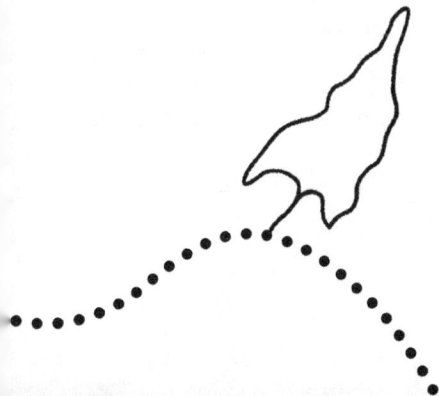

space pancakes from chef Ra

and a beautiful woman in a slinky nightdress sits on a chair
at the opposite side of the breakfast bar to eat
as the ambient fare of electronica music washes out
across the landscape she taps her brightly painted finger
-nails drumming on the plate waiting for something to break
cover, and be revealed in the opening sunshine of the day

chaffinches are quarrelling self-importantly in the horse
-chestnut nearby puffing out their soft pink chests, and firing chirrups
off as if they were mortar rounds at each other oblivious
of the surroundings, breaking, and then darting
back into the shadows the white flashes of their wings
a kind of Morse code signifying something's lost
in translation, the woman pours the coffee that will be her last

feeds the black of it to a cube of white sugar until permeated
a crumbling stone it drops sweet out between
her slender fingers, the droplets sounding a fitting
addition to the timpanic musings of the music in the room as
everything slides casually in a drift of measures,
the grains of sugar nestling amongst the molecules of dark
-water, the chaffinches silenced now in a deep

found within the horse-chestnut leaves, and sleep feels out then after
the little fast has been broken, and sun stretches itself surely now
glares from behind anything that holds its searching
to the loping shadows that crawl and hide away from the headstrong
stare while the house dozing, is an empty stage outside of the colour
or intensity of the suns projections, ghosting heavily in the days round
unsatisfied pull on the chains anchoring them
firmly in place where all that they need is supplied so easily

seeds parachuting from the trees are fine filaments waving
a weave back and fro a trajectory of shivering silver threads, air

uncertainly falling, and just as uncertain, touching on skin

travel a little, death.

At 3 o'clock a black coffee just doesn't do it . . . . .
even with the added sweet energy of honey.

How the battered typewriter monster runs away
in old movies of the fifties and sixties
with the tired hacks typing scripts they had to feed
the machine with, scrolling it in, and under the bar
so the black metal keys hammering against the ribbon
hard pressed the tombstone of each letter
exact and crisp on the paper. How
every page mattered and had to be just so
even though the day had ended and the next was rolling
black as the ribbon pulled across the face of it
that was the stop motion target every key must hit
He typed and simultaneously lit a cigarette
from the dying embers of the last
shouted out for paper
a previously invisible woman somewhere would get
so that the living stream pouring out of him might be captured
thought in its entirety
every wild thing pulled out
named and caged in this way
to change then into something ferociously prowling
margin to margin, contained,
waiting to be fed

Listen

the stands soft roundness's appear
leaves quivered in the making
of a separate

locking down of light

the trees enduring

crowd in common flight
about one tangled toppled form

taken as a fungi sprawl
I would go to see

where the antlers of an aged bared crown

of wrinkled lime
lichen in winter—missing

the way any body might miss
the comradeship of trees

Rome.

Drink a beer, order another
Romulus and Remus as sculptures are
laddish sort of Buddha's,
cherubs drinking at a She-wolf's teats
on individual clouds, while She
hard as hale, simply is
always was, and has no need of a starting place
mythology. Cain and Abel join us.
And then all of those other children raised by wolves.
Until everything dissolves in a language
of the wild, of skins, and all the myths
become insular and incomplete. The Sun
that changeable friend seeks out
escape, rages where some
men sit beer and fags at a small
pale fleshly clothed coloured table.
Peach at a pinch. There is
a chalkboard with today's special
—Cocktail Romoli— fruit(orange/compari/rum/tequila/gin)
chalked up. Across the busy
street waiters at the restaurant set tables.
It is early yet. All
is ordinary. Everyday. What need have we
for myths? Tomorrow I go
to the Pyramid where the train station is,
and on to Ostia and the relentless muscling sea.
It is enough. The Romoli's owner regards us.
Chestnut eyes set in big white skies
call Grandfather who was here in the war.
A serious face the smallest trace of misbehaviour,
anything, could explode, is here.

what was open

so much so that it was starkly revealing
is covered,
                              trees bare frames
clothed what was grey

earth and that stubble things become dying,
                              Cowslip, Nettle, Fern, Dock, Bindweed,
so that everything is softened,
so that the air two Wood pigeons follow each other through is made
apparent

                                            in things
moving, so that what was quiet is
birdcall, insect hum, bees busynesses
of flapping wing feathers down
                   -beat
                         —pushing
                      everything up,
so that all of this rushing to be,
                      of things that happen,
rushes in to us—floods our senses,

so that green, so many variations of green that to call all these greens green

                                      is insufficient,
is overwhelming

a fellow walks up stone steps

a glass door opens
to a circle of doors
to floor upon floor

where a dress of steel needles
too long to be pins
trembles paper forms of birds

they rise up the wall bright colours
flying shadows

a coat of air and wind-
stirs seeds of thistledown
so light that the whiteness is almost

vanished   shoes grow
            on long thin cotton-trees
whose branches undeliver messages

and the sound of a flat blade
vibrates a metal man slung from the roof who suspended
faces the floor on a thick taut wire
the way that you might lower a door
on ropes from a far

fly —man of steel—
hollow inside of the connected ring shell

of yourself
understandably constructed of night
and thought emergent to be overtaken

by kelp-brown leaves that gently turn

the tree has fallen down the hallway
where leaf flight feathers stalling
are fibres are spun

Moth

Splinter of light is a shard shroud clothing what
appears to be a moth laying out on its back, sun-bathed,
legs in the air brittle, hard and sinewy, they might
have felt out, tenderly for sound purchase, found
none. What was a head is shrunken and strangely
extended, drawn out are two thin antenae wires—still
receiving, as crystal radios do, signals in the ether; or
pheromone trails no longer to be followed in fervent hope
of something continuing, in one form, or another, having
already tasted change, and changing again, senselessly,
unfeeling, dried out and broken. Wings are token
wings, gold dustings empty of thrust and propulsion,
are earthbound a confusion of purpose, for
what is it that eats away such spare.

Cuba

Difficult to capture
the hurry and careful
consideration the drivers
of these streets have
Even for strays

And how the strangenesses of place ease
after more than one Mojito

The Teapot Ladies become
familiars in their near Victorian
waitress uniforms, out on patrol
pouring tots of a little something
strong, or even stronger
into small paper cups for
those of us who stand here to watch
the dancers—who also danced
the day before—rehearsing the perfect
Carnival in the square
of Parc Cesperedes

Where the dominoes players are
yellow flowers and thin sails
of seed spiral like helicopters

landing about two girls who squat
beside a cardboard box they've opened up
to release two yellow chicks to the dust

where knarly-teased up tree roots are

Knees hugged tight they wait to see
whether the chicks will run away

Inside the Vedado

district is Parque John Lennon where a life
-size bronze of John sits on a bench leaning

nonchalantly back arm extended   reaching

as if for a thought   I sat
down beside him for a photograph

Suddenly an aged man approached us speaking rapidly
in Spanish   smiling and gesticulating in a friendly

      way
His face, creased and interesting, was animate
with a smile as warm as the sun

He reached into a pocket and brought out John
Lennon's glasses
Carefully fixed them in place on John's face
smiled, and gestured expansively saying
with movement
now all is complete, please sit and I will
take a photograph of the two of you here
in this beautiful place, in the
park beside John.

When we were done he carefully retrieved
John Lennon's glasses, put them safely away

                  and disappeared.

warm silence is

a breeding place of numbers
leading on to Susan's house
whoever Susan is
where the friend we lose turns up lying arms outstretched in the snow
as if crucified
and we empty cans of beer into vases we find
to carry about as precious cargoes
in slack hands
watching as one of the company ridiculously mounts a glass
topped table and goes through
another breaks out through the french windows
glass mingling outside with the crisp snow
that reaches and stretches out minutes so
what we are saying becomes the most important thing
words being strings we must follow or loop around our waists
or wrists
or pass through our ears and pull through one to another
connecting us all together
as everything about us breaks apart
and the future starts
under a hard impact of snow

after all what is there left for us to do?

How the salt affected the cut-wood

air is salt
that is sea
so that the edge where bark
was encrusted dried
like a scab does

ants climb
where it is also dry, but grey, not brown
that brown that is red
as well as brown
the brown of blown sand
of the cliffs rising about here
where land broke and fell away
to join the sea

there is a sand-bar
people wade out to chest high
climb onto and lie
the blue all about
as swells move through from white
to blue, to white again, and then
close in so that brown that is

becomes the colour of cut
-wood crusted through exposure

to the salt in the air

where power chose to frack and burn the climate

Paihia

Sun burns reading Snow on the sand
before a walk through the mangrove swamp
to Haruru Falls where Snapping Shrimp

pop and White Faced Heron daintily-step
about the rocky edges of the shallow pools
where the falling water changes from light
to a pink. The Waitangi

river comes to the end of one
flat, falls, carries on.

Within it multitudinous dank brown
fingers are Strange birds calling
in the voices of others.
                                        Spray blows

    the water descends, and I
catch on to Gorse as spindrift on the way

The humming light

supposes there are as many different kinds of fire
many different kinds of heat
as there are flowers, trees, or insects in a wild.

Carefully observing the tongues of licking
caress and ultimately possess
what it is that feeds

might distinguish between them.
When I was young I often teased
apart the petals, stigma, and stamens

of a flower, fingers becoming stained

bright yellow or orange with pollen.
Bees thinking my hands strange flowers
they had not encountered before

must have burned to dance across the floor
some undecipherable messages of them.

A Second Poem to accompany Du Fa riding on a Donkey.

(by Ikkyo Sojun, 1394-1481)

The man is large
and sideways on
on the unhappy Donkey approaching us
who must be across a stretch
of water it will stretch
its neck down low to sip
ears alertly pricked

The monk looks across over the top
of the Donkeys head toward whatever
approaches beyond the water

His hair is tied in two pigtails
his robes flow from his shoulders
to his gathered toes
impatiently waiting

The working Donkey slows

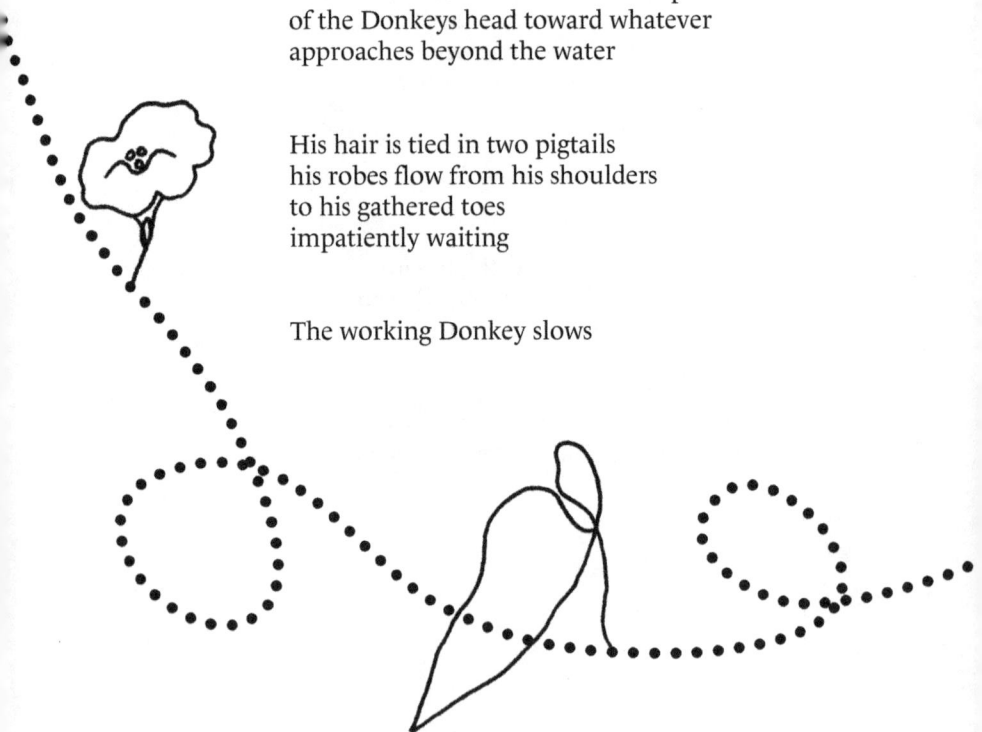

November

read about going to the wrong door late,
thinks about Tom Waits

dancing Spanish, considers Seville,
its Jewish quarter where shade stays close
and as it remembers a fine lace appears
and it considers Morse code—
how once it connected whatever was vital
happening, the now of being at all—

all of these things breathing in this hollow

where soft green moss is such a green
it seems to outshine the idea of itself—is
become a transmission—a stepping off

from the shelves of books where Paul Robeson
becomes once more Old Man River

..where the forced austerity makes good friends redundant....

Three plump Blackbirds come to the window.

Two more hop this way across the dew-wet lawn
One perches atop the slatted backrest of the wooden

bench. They are gone.
Some into the tall dense green of the hedge,
some, that were frenetic fans

in the air, are further away where paths
no longer cross. If I wish,
though I could not make them stay to entertain us

with their hunting and petty squabbles,
I could call them up, dress them in dinner suits
and bow ties, and sit them about the long

fertile table of lush green lawn, where
a breakfast of blood-red early worms and assorted
crunchy insects would make their orderly way

out from the safety of the rain-soaked earth. They
would peck at the food like undertakers at a funeral.
Partaking of everything whilst seeming parsimonious.

One would open its wings and become an old leather
wallet, and out from it notes would be drawn for the waiter
quietly hovering at the edge of the lawn.

Once they had eaten their fill they would all form
a line and march into the air, as if ascending
an invisible stairway, then accelerating

to a short run, open out their wings, and close
them again, as if clapping, and disappear.

So all that remained of them would be the round
echo of applause, resounding, in the air.

Autumn

Flat brittle wrappings shiver and fall.
Red, yellow, and brown temporarily settle the ground, or recoil
in the wind from walking cruncher's, until
downed they form a musty skin
concealing the pavement and bare ribs of land. Their
newness, a quilted statement in the darker days,
defines a space, the gap between man and ground.

Blowing gusts a vivid revolt. Trapped leaves underfoot
a rustling rumour of movement feet hide in,
and rise from, breaking the fresh seal.

A pattern pulled from side to side skimming the earth;

They glide in to softly land and find a place,
just like those walking, head down, fighting the breeze
to go to work in shops and offices,
or in green and yellow all weather overalls work slowly
to brush the fall back and forth into piles, clearing
a space, a path, removing abundance that school

children kick up, and pick up, play dive into,
or throw into the air to see the breeze
take up again, making games content watching as they

pirouette down, until called inside where
the rustling and blowing no longer disturb.

Throwback.

Music hall, show songs, dance bands, symphonies;
obscure oral histories take the day in custody
in a working language, and I'm reassured.

Songs, not mine but taught me,
those renegade genes feelings stirred

returning me to an era that exists
in strange foods stored in tins;

Magical objects with interesting histories;

Lyrical fragments of banjos and mandolins

pull colours, odours, and tastes from memories

hard wired deep within.

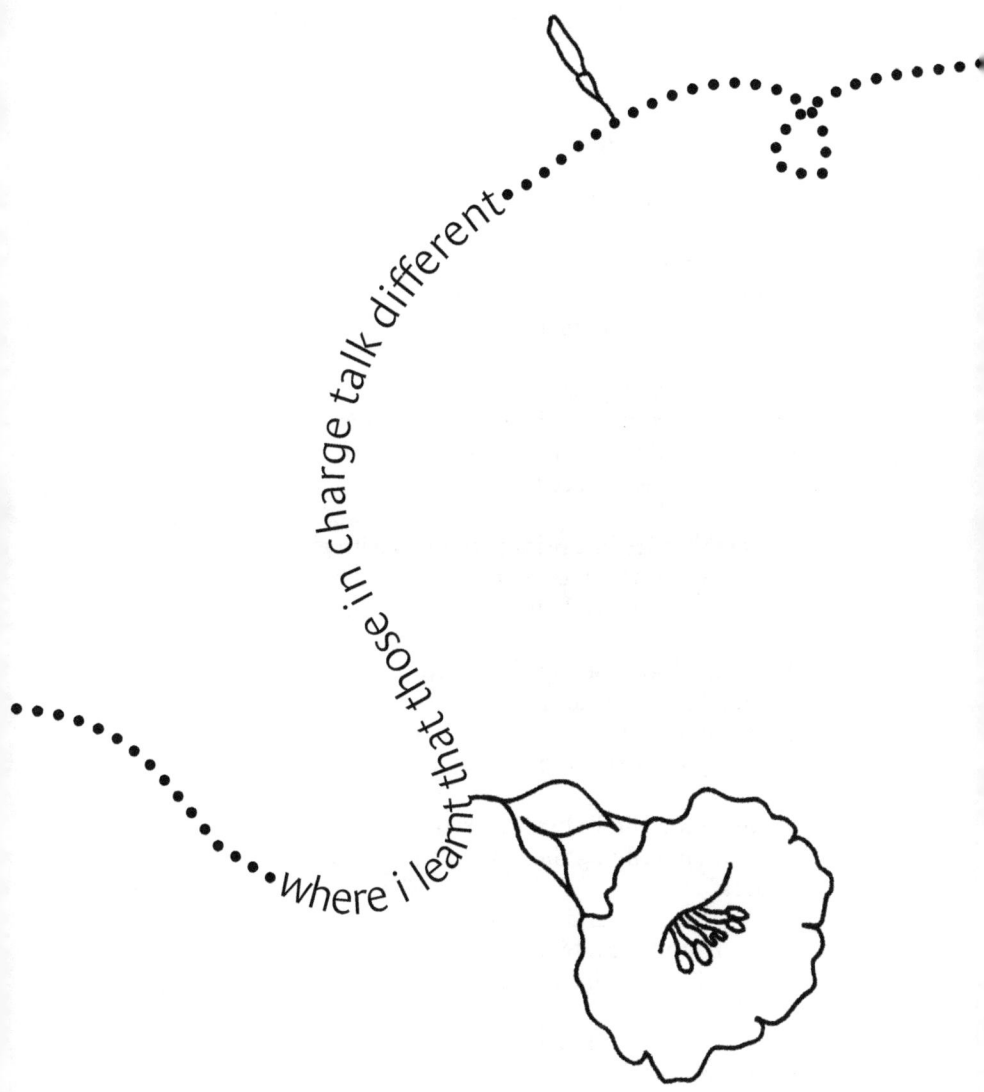

where i learnt that those in charge talk different

Felfeslik (comes unstitched)

(after SATANTANGO—Bela Tarr)

Sight obscured always
is where the land is a flat wet sheet
telling how everything here is mostly
water.
        What
a difference trees make. Leaves,
a layer of riches to dig in, and press
down on,
            stamping
the shoulders of a much-used spade, stooping
to gather and let run through the fingers
a tillage that is replaced

in ways that are like bribing mouths with gifts,
then smoothing out every trace, and scattering
deep about scooped handfuls of leaf mould.

Trees stand so close together they might be thieves
waiting black to black against a darkening sky.
They are remains, remnants, relics even, of a wildfire.
Yet it is you carries a spade like a spear

to where the wind's breath scrapes
everything, scalping the land to a flat waste
of dark,
             and a girl
whose cotton dress billows from under a thick woollen
coat, is climbing through a window into the only building
in existence,
            to escape
the wind, and sit there, watching the dark,
listening to it careening. There is a cat
she finds she caresses under the cracked beam
where she sits.

                    She croons to it
as she fits herself in different ways
into a space beneath the eaves
gaps allow a dim light entrance. The cat whines
the way they do wanting something, attention, food,
warmth perhaps, some comfort, and she croons

some nonsense rhyme that speaks to it, lifting
it bodily by the forelegs so that it hangs limp

as a wet rag, bedraggled as a newly dead thing,
its ears flat back pressed in against its neck in fear,
pliant, supplicant not knowing whether
it will be hurt, yet unable, or unwilling, to struggle.

She holds it up so, gripping the forelegs and shoulders
out away from her body, though it is scared, and would away.
She rolls it over in the dust. Rolls herself with it. Holds

like a vice to its forelegs as it whines,
and twists, but cannot escape.
                                        She lifts

it again and stares expressionless
into its face, brings it close.
                                        Staring.
                                                    As if
they are related to each other, and to the dust, and the beam,
are part of the darkness, and the flat wet land, and the rain.

Dreams

Cut out of a child
the heart bottled in alcohol
placed on a high shelf
and forgotten
was left to dry out

as the alcohol evaporated
it turned
to stone.

Cold stones live
Tell them nothing

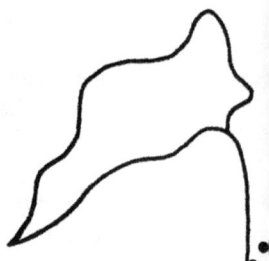

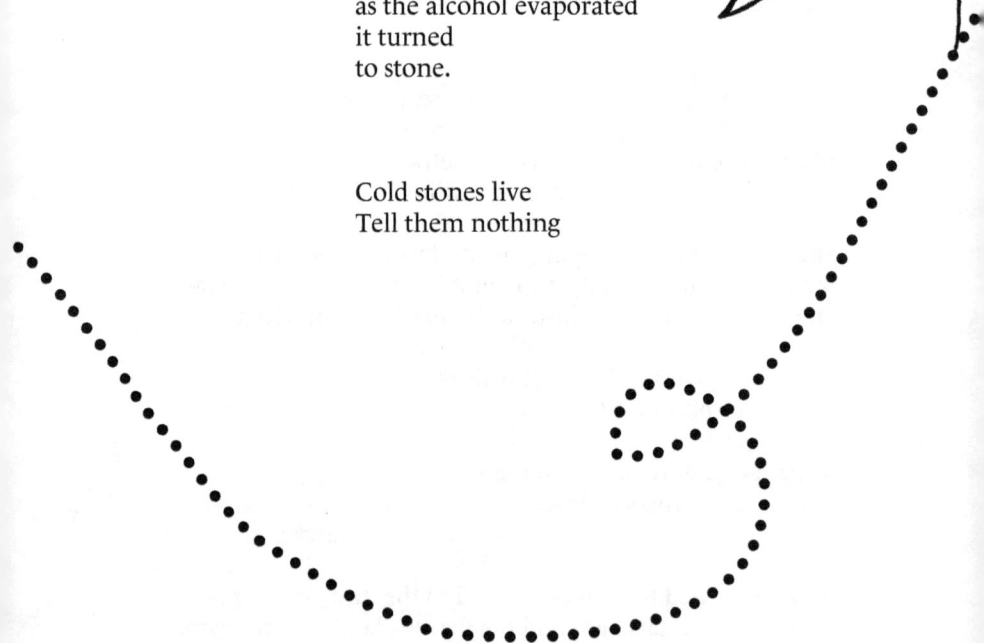

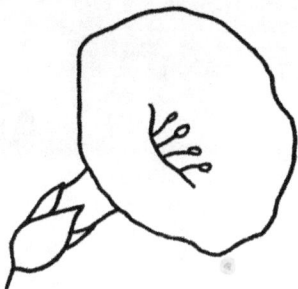

where dreaming is dangerous

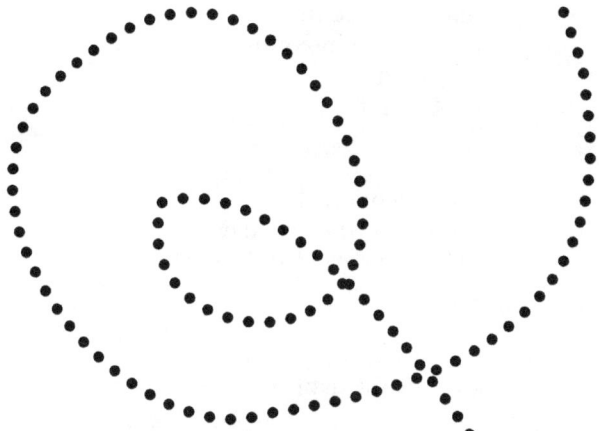

Anger

Doing what I do
splintered the wooden frame
till it could not hold a nail
to the heavy door

to blame
i repair it revoking the anger
that slammed in
harder than intention
wrenching
them apart

until mentioned
cautiously, the next day
as bare feet padded through
cradling tea

viewing the damage

untangling
the words from the grain

Seeing.

outside time I feel
the spin and tender vibration
of molecules, atoms, life

see arcing light on the horizon

measure the pull of it on stems

the orientation of the flowers

how all these are within orbits

do not count minutes or hours

separations of skin dissolve

fragment, and begin, just begin
to scatter, as atoms, molecules

soil grows, and is pulled
to new skies about another sun

ape eye stars have not yet spun

Passed on

He'd make things from the foil
wrappings while we drank our coffees, ate our sweets.

He'd make a chalice, or a small bird, a man, or some such
to stand fragile in a shining

crinkled skin upon the table

patiently waiting for us to finish.

Now she makes them, his skill
passed. Twisting the delicate foil
taking care not to rip it.

Fashioning a base that'll hold
it upright there, safe and still.

I watch her fingers working this material,
her concentration lighting it.

See the smile of achievement as she sets
down the newly sculpted form

having lifted it to her lips
to breathe brief life to it

or perhaps to kiss

What are the words again?

Know that i did not want to hear that song
for it moved inside me
crocus lipped
delicately inked as a shaded poppy
copiously and conscientiously copied
inaccurately disassembled and reassembled
it was a new thing, and any
replaying of the original would disappoint, or prove dull

within the hush

a history of clearings
damped down meadows
borders made
of grass and nettle
crossed recrossed
by wild dew
curled tips
of inwardness

of springs and trips of
multiplications where
carbon flowers are
shy blue and butter

here each overflows
the notes of itself

clouds roll fields
and the sun breaking
is a waking

glow

high above, higher than any could conceive of
mastiff star receivers fiery tree wound captioned night
enfolds the befouled earth
and in a capriciousness of sea moving
moon journeying, and shine
a constellation littered ocean, and beyond
a land where wind moving trees chafe
shadow dark and darker

oh england's

where i was placed in the driving seat of a dumper truck aged three
where for almost a year i assembled jigsaws, drew birds, and played in sand
where for a dare we would walk the joists of new builds
where we found a way in to the cricketer's hut through the floor boards
where i would ride a bike no hands down the steepest hill
where from nowhere the eleven plus exam loomed to divide us
where mother worked as a typist in the mills
where granddad once called to our house to read the meter
where my brothers followed me when they started school
where i left a good friend to pass to the grammer
where i walked school mornings to a friends who had no dad
where others shouted paki at me as i walked
where i never figured out what i wanted to do
where i was taught that you had to work
where zero hour contracts now exist
where my father had to leave school at fourteen to work
where his father had to leave school at twelve to work
where we moved from a small terrace on beechgrove ave at five
where i sat on a pot toadstool left at the nursery at three
where we played football english against pakis
where penny showed me all the way to the tops of her coloured tights
where i was made aware that—a Buttercup
                                  a Thrush
                                      Water
                                          warm of Sun
                       even the most imperceptible
                   small part
                           of an inhalation, or
                                          exhalation—a thought
                                  even the genes
                 that direct the forming of us—have a price
             and that that price is all that matters
where when the Grandchildren are happy—so am i

where there is never enough money
                              for the National Health, or Welfare, or
                         Social Services, or Education, or any caring thing
where unlimited money was found and made to prop up failing banks
where we are told it would be wrong to limit the pay of those who get most
where we are told there is no money to pay more than the minimum wage

where i learnt a taught history and about other countries
where when i could i ran and when i couldn't run i fought

where history was a photo of a man with melting eyes

where i realised that reason doesn't win
where i was told i was wrong even when i was right

where i studied biology not knowing why
where we protested and a good friend standing right beside me was arrested
where there are cameras everywhere
where the job for life disappeared

where the phones we pay for tell others where we are and what we say
where at a good friends trial the camera that caught his innocence didn't
work

where three police officers lied under oath
                                        and nothing was done
where i learnt to distrust money

where i realised i never really knew my grandmother
where my granddad, grandma, granddad, auntie, uncle, and on, and on . . . died
where one of my three daughters was born
where my Mother still lives because of the National Health

where the o level results were announced to the class, and most cried
where only two of us could carry on at school
where the three rivers burst their banks and flood came
where i learnt not to trust newspapers
where waters rose so that we moved from Broad Street to the top of a hill

where if you can pay your child's school can have small class sizes
                                                    and a theatre
                                                    and a music studio
                                        every conceivable instrument
                            and every child will have a laptop
                                                        that works
                                        and can play every type of sport
                        and re-take exams until they get the results
            to go where they want to—to do what they want
where power chose to frack and burn the climate
where i marched against an unnecessary war
where we sent an army to fight that war
where we made the weapons that destroyed the cities
                                        the water plants
                                        the electricity
                                            the hospitals
                made homeless the men women and children
            widowed and orphaned
                                        making obscene profits

where i liked how smooth rounded cobbles warmed bare feet in summer
where ice cream used to be solid and yellow and vanilla sweet
where what was Spring Summer Autumn Winter is no longer
where i go out from
where the powers that be stealthily privatised our National Health

where power put businessmen in charge of our children's schools
where i had the best ever fish and chips at Staithes, aged eleven
where forced austerity makes friends redundant
where i became a vegetarian

where i would be chased and hugged by big west Indian girls in the factory
where girls in blowmoulding wore just a bra and pants under their protective
                                                                              clothing
where i found that skiving in mary's pantry became boring
where i drank brains, no that was wales

where i would gather bucket's full of frogs, newts, and toads—and put them
                                                                              back

where the powers that be took us to an illegal war
where the leader that took us to war became a millionaire
                               and was then appointed an envoy for peace

where from top pond down to the low by Rickerty Bridge have all been drained

where freedom is defined as having a choice at the shops

where i learnt that those in charge talk different
                               and that i am judged by how i talk

where kathy smiled and i lost my heart . . . no that was Scotland

where the computers we buy tell others whatever we do
                                                 spying for them

where power tells us we are free
where electricity costs more if you can't pay

where freedom really exists for those with money
where years after the illegal war a report tells us it was unnecessary
                            that all those deaths were a waste
                            that attacking countries was wrong
where i feel less safe

where for all my adult life there was no-one i believed in to vote for
where unexpectedly i became a poet
where i moved my wife and children to
where i think of moving away from

where dreaming is dangerous

where those in charge never stand trial
where i found that the law works for big money

where i learnt that those at the top most often know nothing

or pretend to

where i question everything

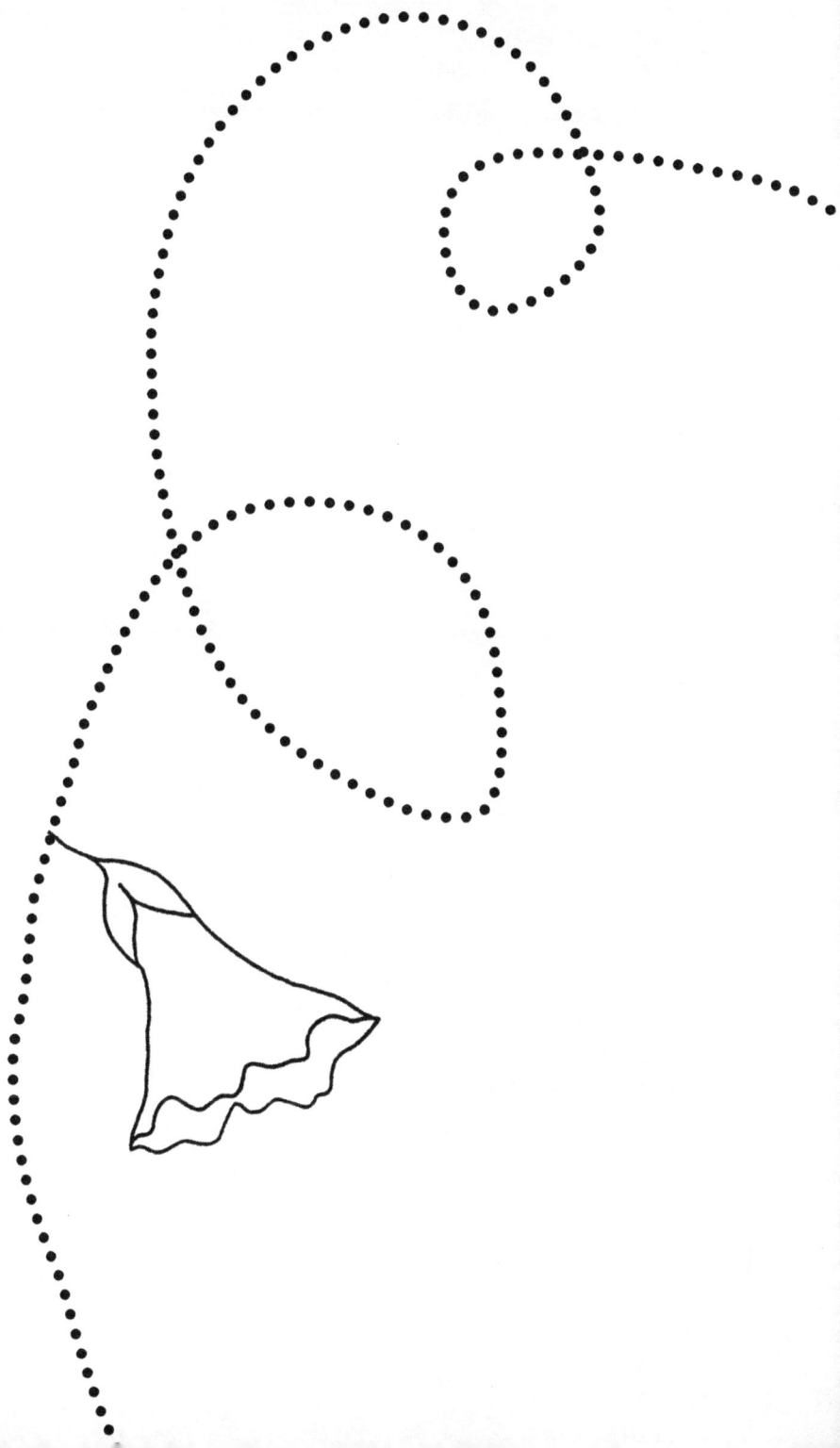

III

before she was named Ava

a bird nested
in the chimney breast.

hear it
side-to-siding
early every morning.

she rests
the flat of a hand on the solid
kick inside

while there is light there is singing

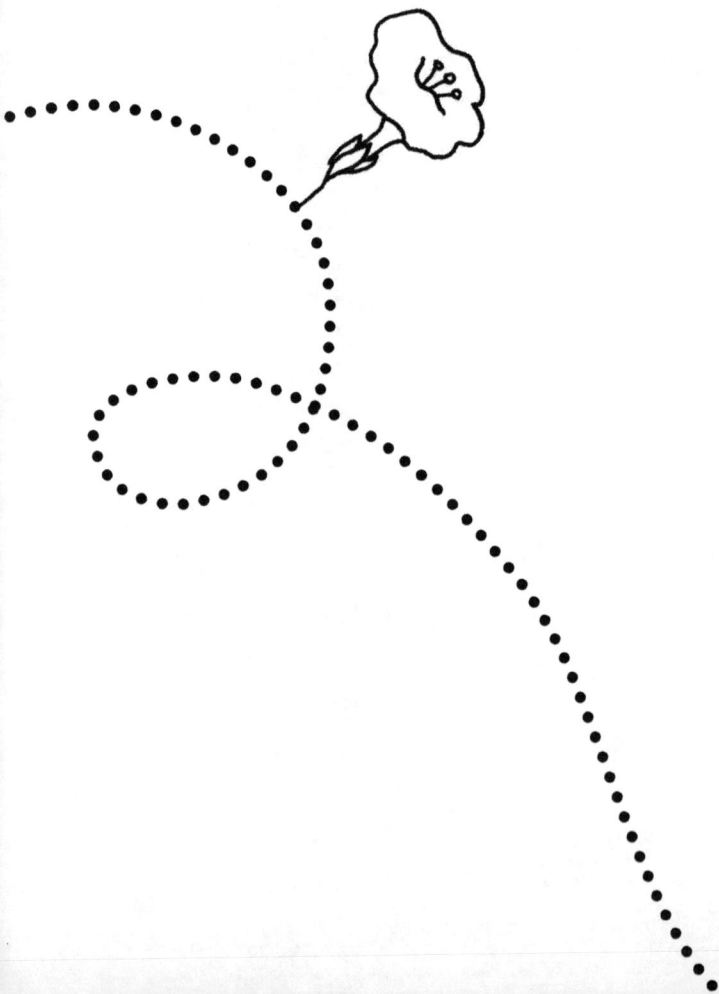

poetry & haiku titles from The Onslaught Press

SNEACHTA (2016) Gabriel Rosenstock

THE LIGHTBULB HAS STIGMATA (2016) Helen Fletcher

OUT OF THE WILDERNESS (2016) by Cathal Ó Searcaigh
with an introduction and translations by Gabriel Rosenstock

YOU FOUND A BEATING HEART (2016) Nisha Bhakoo

I WANNA MAKE JAZZ TO YOU (2016) Moe Seager

TEA WI THE ABBOT (2016) Scots haiku by John McDonald
with transcreations in Irish by Gabriel Rosenstock

JUDGEMENT DAY (2016) Gabriel Rosenstock

WE WANT EVERYTHING (2016) Moe Seager

TO KINGDOM COME (2016) edited by Rethabile Masilo

THE LOST BOX OF EYES (2016) Alan John Stubbs

ANTLERED STAG OF DAWN (2015) Gabriel Rosenstock,
with translations by Mariko Sumikura & John McDonald

BEHIND THE YEW HEDGE (2015) Mathew Staunton & Gabriel Rosenstock

BUMPER CARS (2015) Athol Williams

WASLAP (2015) Rethabile Masilo

AISTEAR ANAMA (2014) Tadhg Ó Caoinleáin

FOR THE CHILDREN OF GAZA (2014)
edited by Mathew Staunton & Rethabile Masilo

POISON TREES (2014) Philippe Saltel & Mathew Staunton